1·2·3 Draw
People

A step-by-step guide by
Freddie Levin

Peel Productions, Inc
Vancouver WA

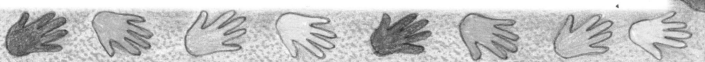

You will need:

- a pencil
- an eraser (one of my most important art supplies!)
- a pencil sharpener
- lots of paper (recycle and re-use)
- colored pencils for finishing drawings
- a folder for saving your work
- a good light
- a comfortable place to draw

Now let's begin!

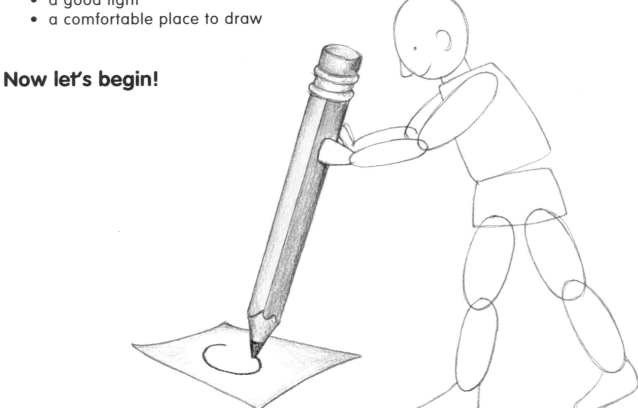

Published by Peel Productions, Inc.
Printed in China

Library of Congress Cataloging-in-Publication Data

Levin, Freddie.
  1-2-3 draw people / by Freddie Levin.
      p. cm.
  Includes index.
  ISBN 0-939217-63-5 (pbk. : alk. paper)
  1. Human figure in art--Juvenile literature. 2. Colored pencil drawing--
Technique--Juvenile literature. I. Title. II. Title: One-two-three draw
people. III. Title: Draw people.

  NC765.L41 2007
  704.9'42--dc22

                    2006024867

Distributed to the trade and art
markets in North America by

NORTH LIGHT BOOKS,
an imprint of F&W Publications, Inc.
4700 East Galbraith Road
Cincinnati, OH 45236

(800) 289-0963

Contents

Important Drawing Tips:

1 Draw lightly at first (SKETCH), so you can erase extra lines later.

2 The first few shapes are important. LOOK at the size, shape and positions of the first shapes.

3 To shade and color your drawing, start lightly and GRADUALLY make the color darker. Don't forget you can BLEND colors too.

4 Practice, practice, practice!

5 Have fun drawing people!

Basic shapes

The drawings in this book all begin with a few basic shapes. Learn these shapes and practice drawing them.

square

rectangle

triangle

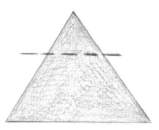

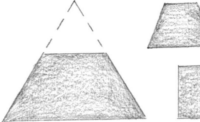

A **trapezoid** is a triangle with the top cut off.

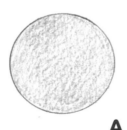

A

B

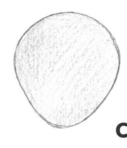

C

A   A circle fits in a square
B   An oval fits in a rectangle.
C   An egg shape fits in a trapezoid. We will be using lots of egg shapes for drawing heads.

Remember:

1   Draw lightly at first - SKETCH.
2   Practice.
3   Practice.
4   Practice.
5   Have fun drawing PEOPLE.

Drawing people

Let's look at some of the basic shapes and proportions for drawing people. We'll get into details later.

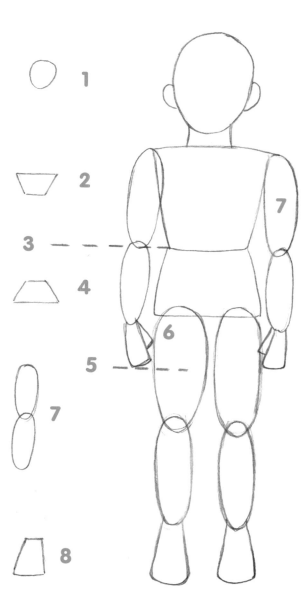

1 The head is egg shaped.

2 The chest is a trapezoid.

3 Put your arms down at your sides. Notice elbows are at the waist.

4 From the waist to the beginning of the legs is the second trapezoid.

5 Put your hands down at your sides. Notice your hands are at the middle of your thighs.

6 Notice your hand. Your thumb is on the inside.

7 Arms and legs are ovals. They are connected at elbows and knees.

8 The basic shape of hands and feet is a trapezoid.

Basic person
front view

Before we draw people in action, we will draw some basic figures. All the people in this book start the same way, head first.

1 Draw an egg shape for the head.

2 Add curved lines for ears. Draw two lines for the neck.

3 Draw a trapezoid for the chest.

4 Add a second trapezoid to complete the lower body.

5 Draw ovals for the upper arms and legs.

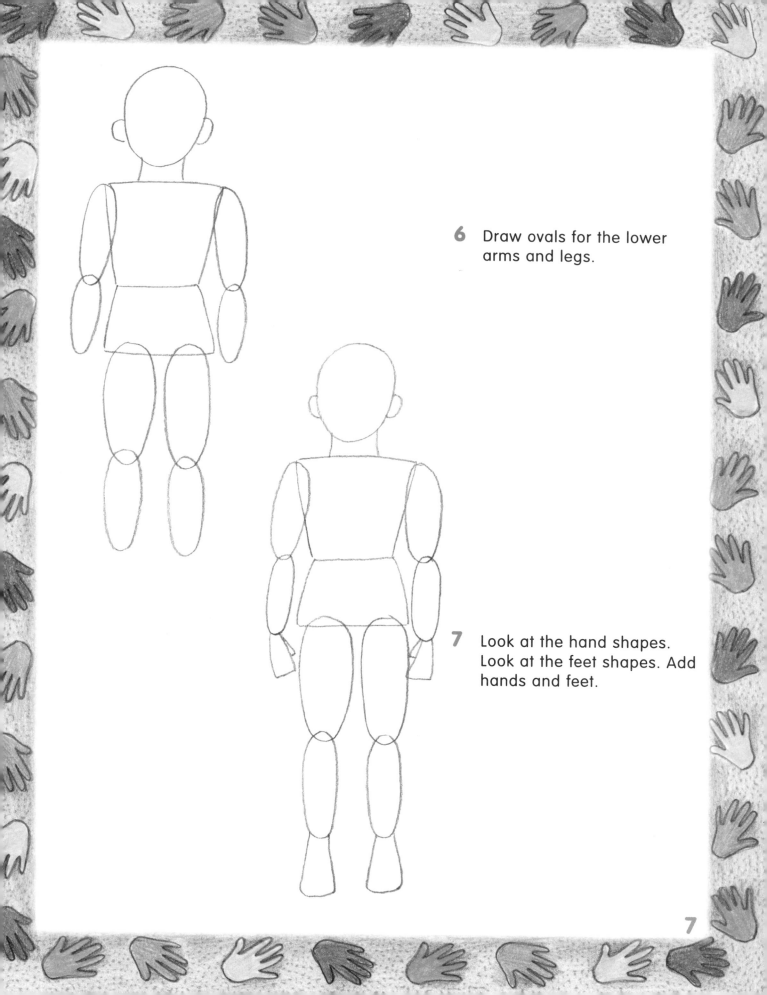

6 Draw ovals for the lower arms and legs.

7 Look at the hand shapes. Look at the feet shapes. Add hands and feet.

7

Basic person
side view

A side view of a head is called a **profile**.

1 Notice the angle of the egg shape. It is different from the front view of the head. Sketch it.

2 Add two neck lines.

3 Look at the chest shape. Notice that it is a different trapezoid shape than the front view. Draw the chest.

4 Look at the lower body trapezoid. Draw it.

5 This person is walking so the arms and legs are swinging out away from the body. Look at the ovals. Draw the upper arms and legs.

6 Look at the lower arm and leg ovals. Draw these.

7 Look at the hand shapes. Notice the thumb location. Add hands and feet.

Even though the arms and legs are moving away from the body, the proportion of the figure is the same. Elbows meet the waist. Hands come to mid-thighs.

Proportion

To make a drawing of a person look natural, it has to be in proportion.

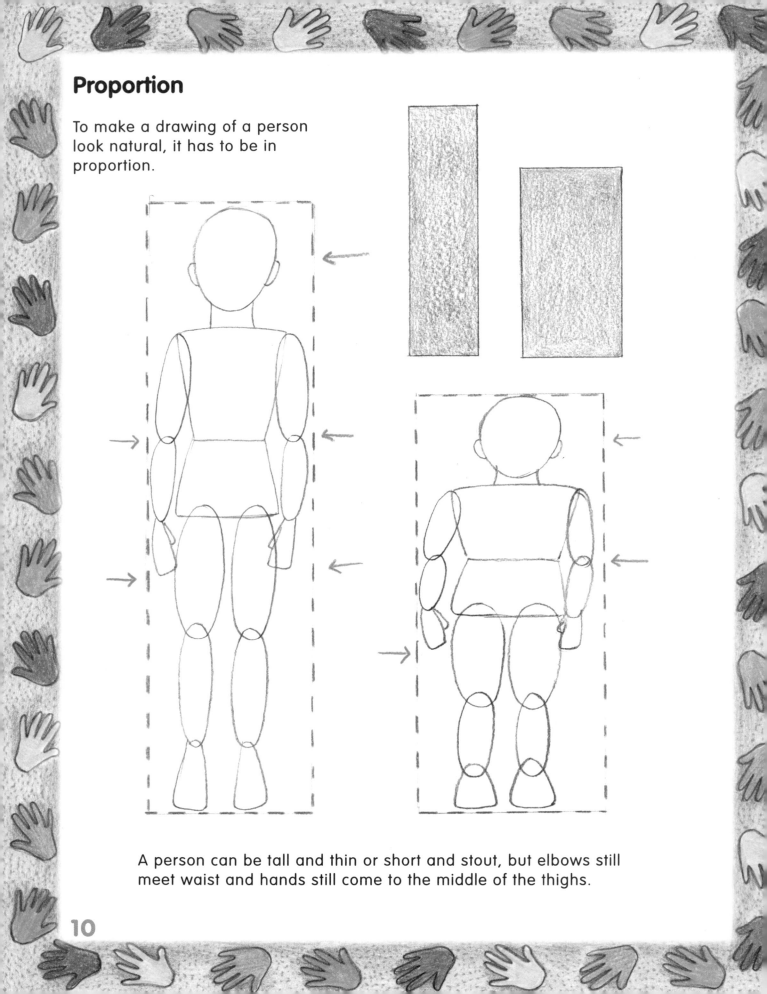

A person can be tall and thin or short and stout, but elbows still meet waist and hands still come to the middle of the thighs.

The face
front view

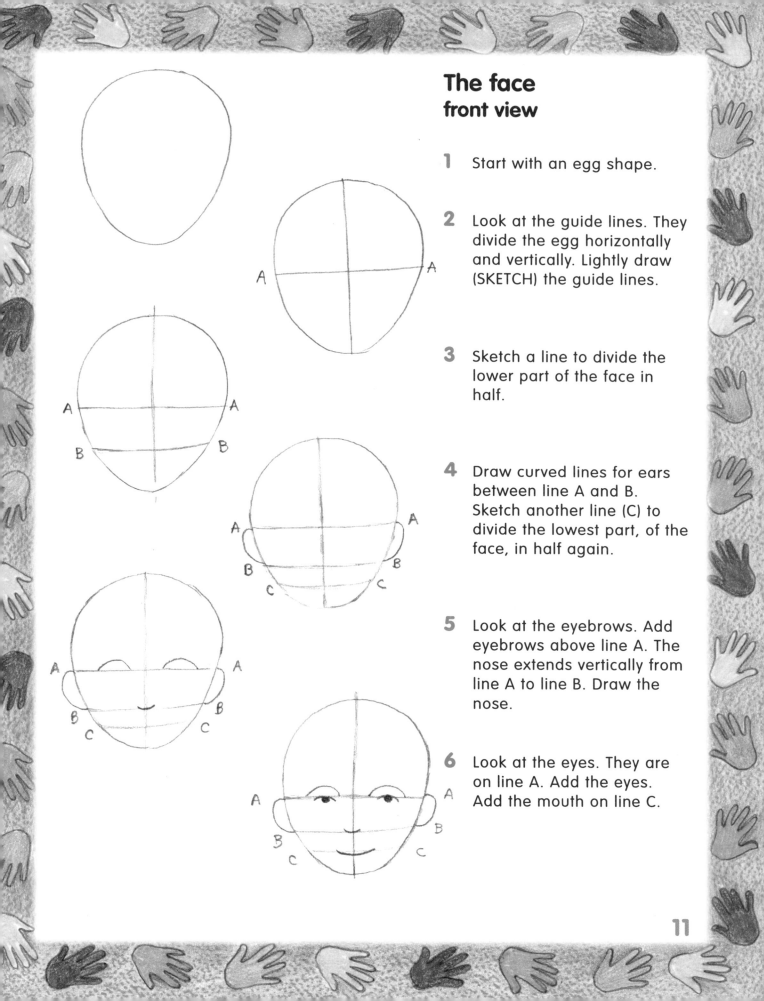

1 Start with an egg shape.

2 Look at the guide lines. They divide the egg horizontally and vertically. Lightly draw (SKETCH) the guide lines.

3 Sketch a line to divide the lower part of the face in half.

4 Draw curved lines for ears between line A and B. Sketch another line (C) to divide the lowest part, of the face, in half again.

5 Look at the eyebrows. Add eyebrows above line A. The nose extends vertically from line A to line B. Draw the nose.

6 Look at the eyes. They are on line A. Add the eyes. Add the mouth on line C.

Look at these different, front view, facial expressions. Notice the eye and mouth lines. Eyebrow lines are also important to expressions. Look in a mirror and make different expressions. Ask a friend to model some. Try drawing the expressions you see.

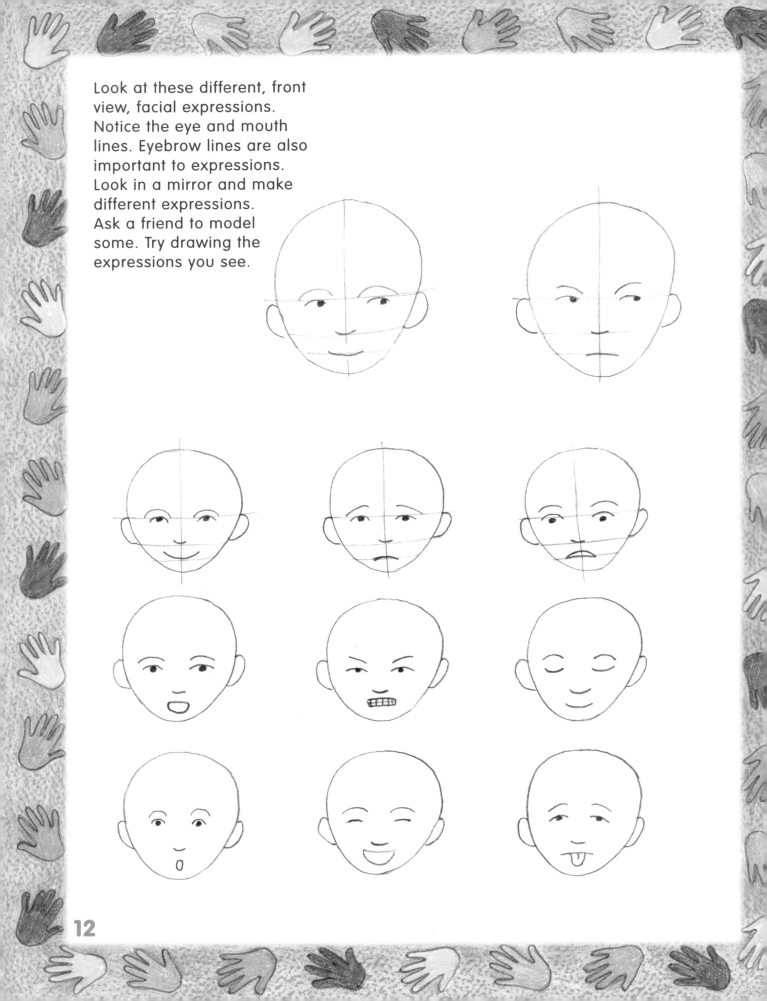

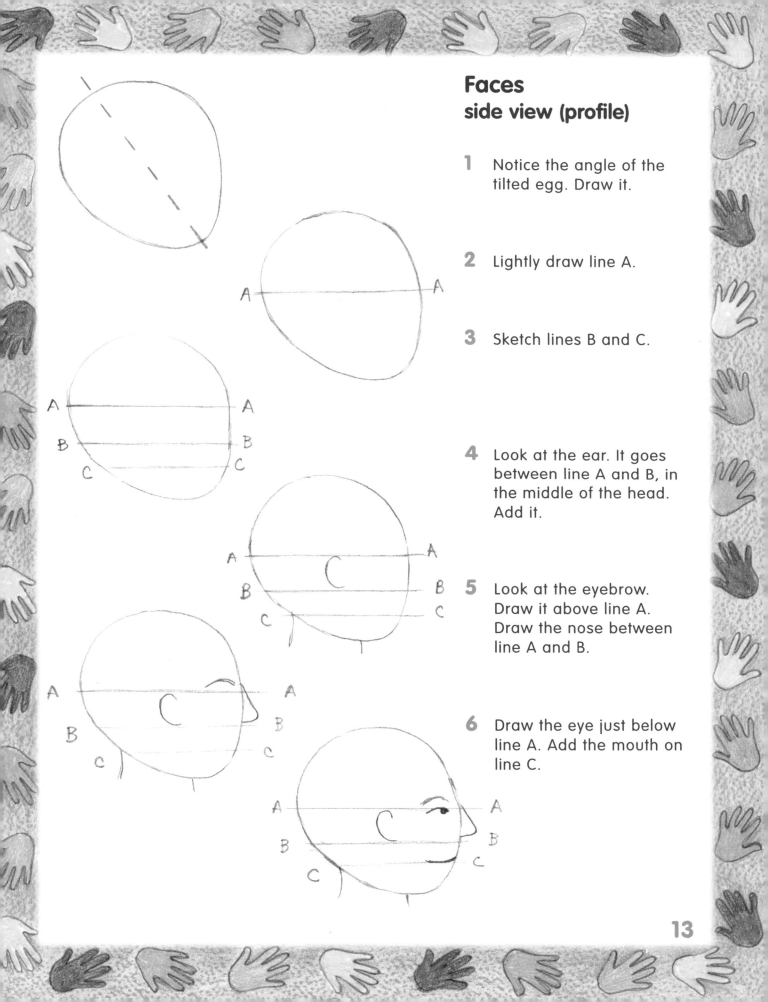

Faces
side view (profile)

1 Notice the angle of the tilted egg. Draw it.

2 Lightly draw line A.

3 Sketch lines B and C.

4 Look at the ear. It goes between line A and B, in the middle of the head. Add it.

5 Look at the eyebrow. Draw it above line A. Draw the nose between line A and B.

6 Draw the eye just below line A. Add the mouth on line C.

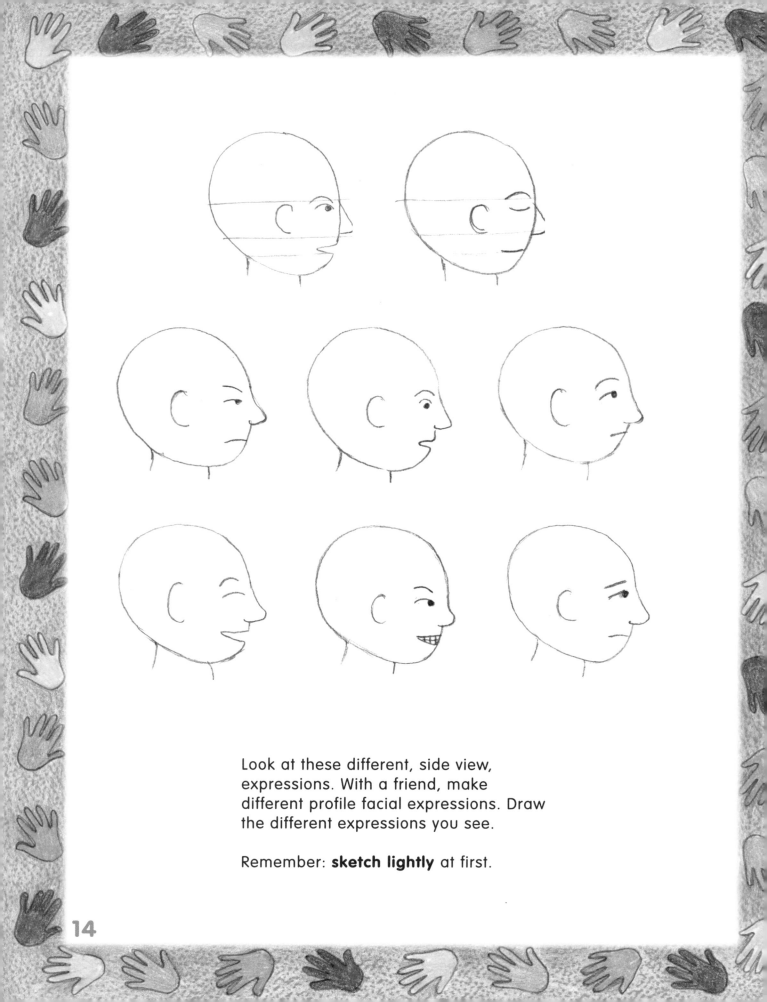

Look at these different, side view, expressions. With a friend, make different profile facial expressions. Draw the different expressions you see.

Remember: **sketch lightly** at first.

Hands

Here are two simple ways to draw a hand.

1 Look at the first trapezoid. Draw it.

2 Add another trapezoid on top.

3 Look at the finger lines. Draw lines to divide the top trapezoid into four fingers.

4 Look at the thumb shape. Add a thumb. Erase extra lines.

1 Start with a trapezoid.

2 Add a thumb

3 Add four fingers.

4 Erase extra lines.

Good Job!

15

Feet

Front view of a foot:

1 Look at the trapezoid shape. This is a longer shape than the trapezoid you used for a hand. Draw it.

2 Remember: the 'big toe' is bigger than the rest! Add four short toe lines.

3 Round off the shape of the toes. Erase extra lines.

4 Add toenails.

Side view of a foot:

1 Start with a triangle.

2 Add two lines for the ankle.

3 Round off the shape of the foot. Erase extra lines.

4 Draw the curves on the bottom of the foot.

Skin color

People come in a range of colors, from light peach to dark brown and every shade in between.

Draw the outline of several hands. Use your colored pencils to blend different skin colors. Remember, even if you decide to make all your people blue and green and purple, that's okay. Art is about observation and imagination. That means you can draw things that you see and you can also draw things that you make up.

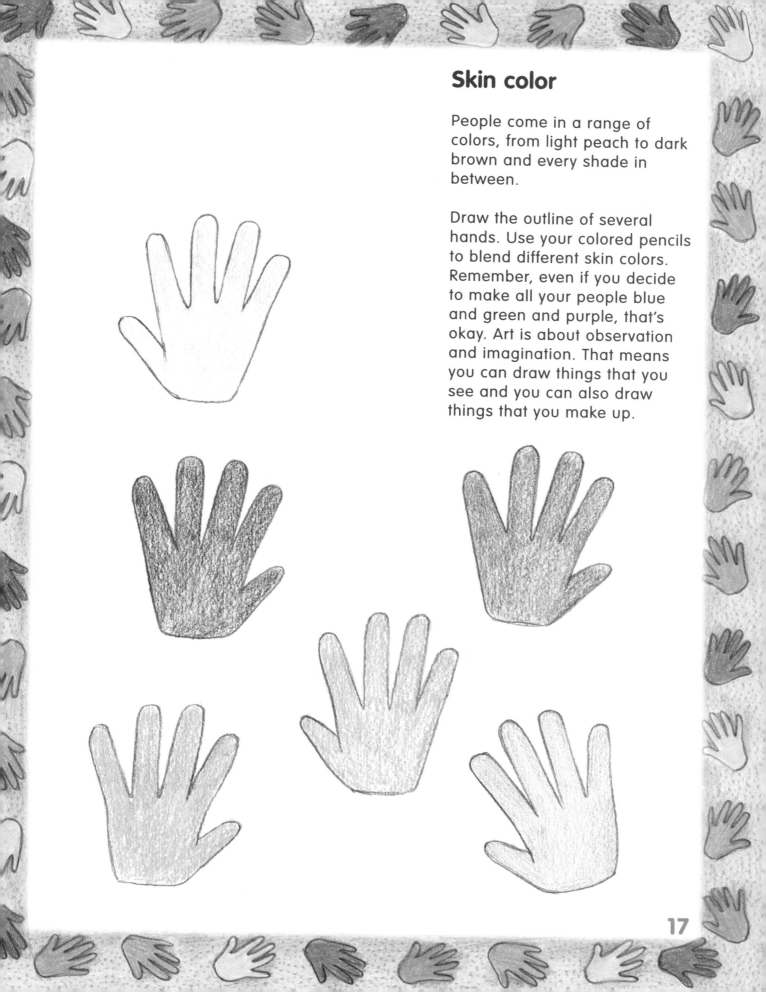

Hair

People have straight hair, curly hair, or wavy hair. Hair can be blond or red or brown or black. People wear their hair long or short or loose or braided. Hair can be spiky or smooth. Some people add beads and bows and barrettes to their hair. Some people dye their hair crazy colors like hot pink or green or blue. Look at the people around you and notice what their hair is like.

Now that you have practiced faces, draw a picture of yourself (SELF PORTRAIT). Look in a mirror or at a photograph of yourself. What is your hair color? What is your eye color? What is your skin color? Is your nose big or small? Do you have freckles or rosy cheeks? Do you wear glasses? Do you have a favorite hat? Draw a portrait of yourself then draw portraits of your friends and family.

Boy running

Now that you know how to draw a basic person, let's add ACTION. Each person, boy or girl, starts with basic shapes. You can give your person any color of skin, hair, or clothes that you want.

1 Draw an egg shape for the head.

2 Add two lines for the neck.

3 Look at the chest shape. Draw the chest.

4 Look at the bottom shape. Draw the bottom of the body.

5 Look at the ovals that begin the arms and legs. Add these.

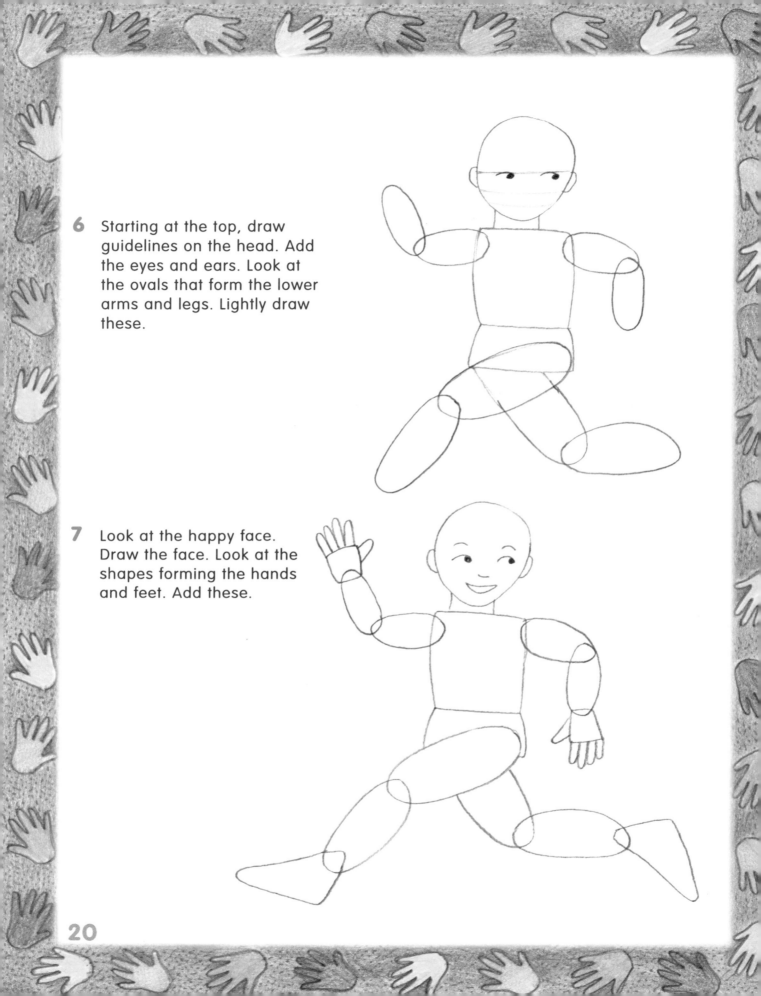

6 Starting at the top, draw guidelines on the head. Add the eyes and ears. Look at the ovals that form the lower arms and legs. Lightly draw these.

7 Look at the happy face. Draw the face. Look at the shapes forming the hands and feet. Add these.

20

8 Look closely at this drawing. Starting at the top, draw the hair. Add arm lines. Draw the clothes. Erase extra lines.

9 Shade and color your running person.

Ballet dancer

Ballet is a form of dance that takes many years of serious training and hard work.

1   Start with an egg for the head.

2   Add two neck lines.

3   Draw the chest trapezoid.

4   Add ears. Notice the angle of the second body trapezoid. Draw it.

5   Look at the angles of the upper arm and leg ovals. Draw these.

6 Look at the dancer's face. Draw the face. Draw the lower ovals of the arms and legs.

7 Starting at the top, look closely at the hair. Draw hair. Notice the position of the left hand. It is drawn to show her holding a wand. Draw the hands. Look at the feet shapes. Female ballet dancers wear special toe shoes so they can dance on the tips of their toes. Draw the feet.

23

8 Look closely at the ballet dancer, head to toe. Starting at the top, add hair and the wand. Draw the ballet dancer's costume. Her skirt is called a 'tutu'. Add lines for her ballet shoes. Erase extra lines.

9 Shade and color your ballet dancer.

Delightful dancer!

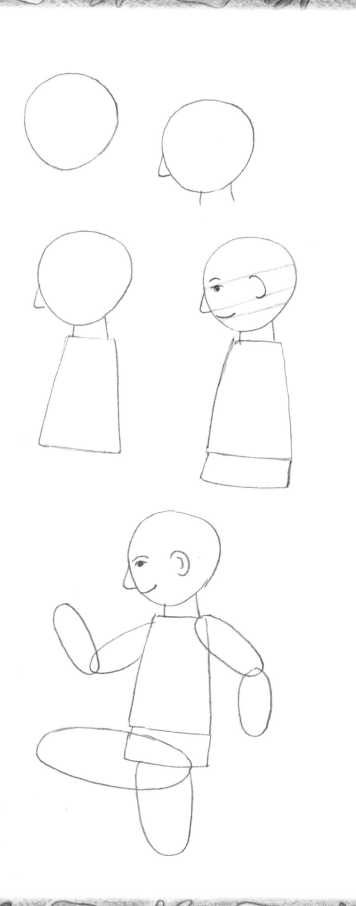

Soccer player

Soccer is a popular sport all over the world.

1 Start with an egg shape for the head.

2 Add two neck lines. Draw the nose. This face will be in profile.

3 Draw a trapezoid for the chest.

4 Lightly draw guidelines for the facial features. Add the eyebrow, eye, ear, and mouth. Draw the lower body trapezoid.

5 Look closely at the angles of the arm and leg ovals. Draw these. Erase the face guidelines.

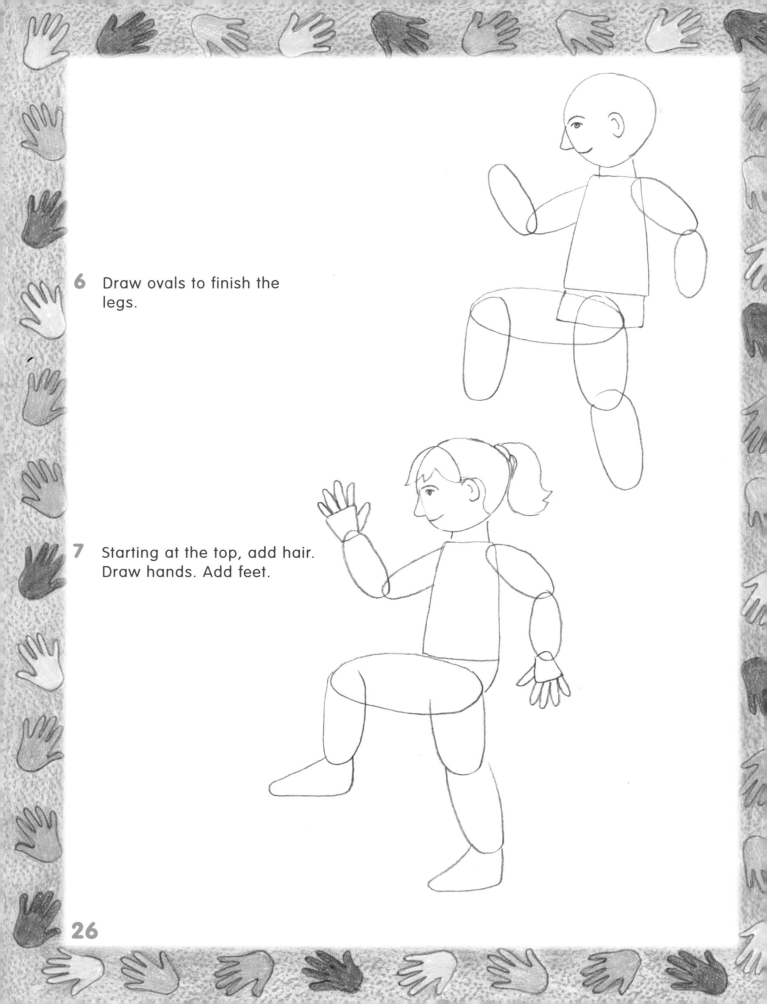

6 Draw ovals to finish the legs.

7 Starting at the top, add hair. Draw hands. Add feet.

26

8 Look at the details on this uniform. Draw the soccer player's team uniform. Erase extra lines.

9 Shade and color your soccer player.

Long ago, my uncle played for the British team, Manchester United. Go Man-U!

Martial Arts

Most of the familiar forms of martial arts, such as Karate or Judo, originated in Asia. The color of the belt tells how high a rank a student has achieved.

1   Notice the angle of the head. Draw the head.

2   Add the face and ear.

3   Notice the angle of the chest trapezoid. Add two lines for the neck. Draw the chest.

4   Notice the angle of the bottom trapezoid. Draw it.

5   Look at the position of the arm and leg ovals. Draw these.

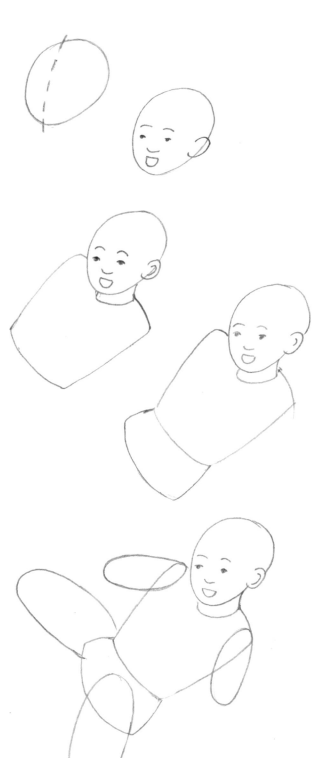

6 Look at the angle of the lower arm and leg ovals. Draw these.

7 Look at the position of the hands and feet. This move is called a sidekick. Draw the hands and feet. His feet are bare.

8 Look closely, head to toes. Draw the hair. The jacket is called a "gi" (GEE as in GARDEN). Add the jacket, pants, and belt. Draw lines for fingers and toes. Erase extra lines.

9 Shade and color your person. What color would you like the belt to be?

Gymnast

The movements of gymnastics are designed to show strength, agility, and flexibility. This girl is learning a walkover, on a practice beam which is only a few inches off the floor.

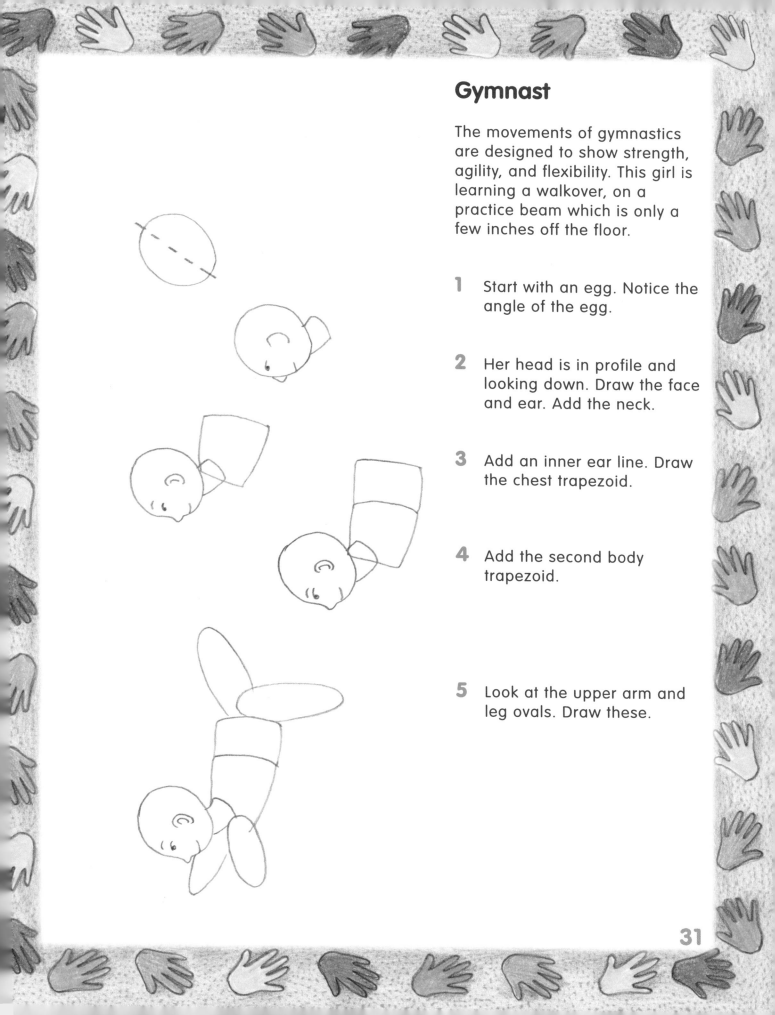

1 Start with an egg. Notice the angle of the egg.

2 Her head is in profile and looking down. Draw the face and ear. Add the neck.

3 Add an inner ear line. Draw the chest trapezoid.

4 Add the second body trapezoid.

5 Look at the upper arm and leg ovals. Draw these.

6 Draw the lower arm and leg ovals.

7 Look closely at the position of the feet and hands. Notice the position of the thumbs. Add hands. Draw feet. Her feet are bare.

8 Gymnasts usually tie their hair back or wear it short, so it does not get in their way. Draw hair. Draw her team uniform. Erase extra lines.

9 Shade and color your gymnast. Draw her practice balance beam.

Great Gymnast!

Baseball player

Baseball is America's national sport. It is hard to imagine summer without it.

1 Let's draw the batter. Start with an egg.

2 Look at the face. Notice that it is a 3/4 view. Draw the face and ear.

3 Draw the neck and chest.

4 Add the second body trapezoid.

5 Look at the position of the upper arm and leg ovals. Draw these.

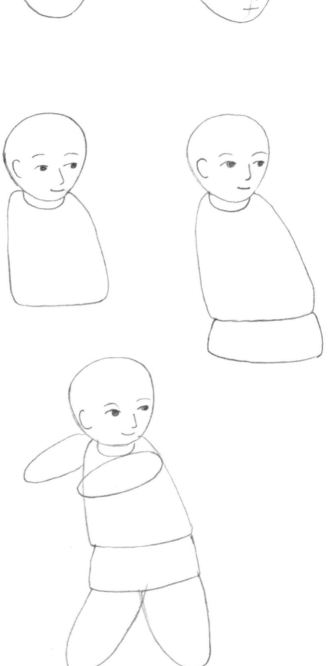

6 Draw the lower arm and leg ovals.

7 Look carefully at the position of the hands. Draw the hands. Add the feet.

8 Look at the special protective hat. It's called a batting helmet. Draw it. Add a tee shirt, pants, and shoes. Draw the beginning of the bat. Erase extra lines.

9 Finish drawing the bat. Shade and color your baseball player.

Yoga

This boy is practicing yoga, an ancient system of exercises that help with strength, flexibility, and balance. This pose is called 'Tree'.

1 Draw an egg.

2 Draw the face and ears. Notice the eyes. They are drawn to show him looking down.

3 Draw the neck and chest.

4 Add the second trapezoid to finish the body.

5 Draw the upper arm and leg ovals.

6 Look at the position of the arm and leg ovals. Draw these.

7 Look at the hand and feet shapes. Draw these.

8 Look closely, top to bottom. Draw hair. Draw his shirt and pants. Erase extra lines.

9 Shade and color your boy practicing yoga.

Yoga is usually practiced barefoot on a special rubber mat.

Ice Skater

Figure skating is one of the most graceful sports to watch. Skaters practice long hours to make it look so smooth and easy.

1   Start with an egg.

2   Draw the face. Add two lines for the neck.

3   Draw the chest trapezoid.

4   Look at the tilt of the second trapezoid. Draw it.

5   Look at the ovals beginning the upper arms and legs. Draw these.

6 Add hair. Draw the ovals for the lower arms and legs.

7 Look at the outstretched hands. Draw them. Begin drawing the skates with triangle shapes.

8 Starting at the top, look closely at the ice skater's outfit. Draw her hair. Draw her outfit, the boots of the skates, and the blades. Erase extra lines.

9 Shade and color your ice skater.

Smooth skater!

Skateboarder

A skateboard is just a board on wheels, but skateboarders can do some amazing tricks on them. Wear your helmet!

1   This head will be in profile. Draw an egg.

2   Add a nose. Draw two lines for the neck.

3   Draw a trapezoid for the chest.

4   Draw the eye and mouth. Finish the lower body with a second trapezoid.

5   Draw ovals for the upper arms and legs.

6 Draw ovals for the lower arms and legs.

7 Look at the outstretched hands. Draw the hands. Look at the feet and skateboard. Draw the feet and skateboard.

8 Head to toe, look at the details. Add a helmet and hair, and other details you see. Erase extra lines.

9 Shade and color your skateboarder.

Super skateboarder!

45

Bicyclist

Bicycles are a great way to get around. People use bicycles all around the world.

Bicycles are complicated to draw. Let's take it slow, step by step.

1 This head will be in profile. Start with an egg.

2 Draw the ear, face and nose. Add lines for the neck.

3 Draw the chest trapezoid.

4 Notice how the lower trapezoid is tilted. Draw it.

5 Look at the position of the upper arm and leg ovals. Draw these.

6 Draw the ovals for the lower arms. Add hands. Draw the lower leg shapes and one foot.

7 Draw a helmet and hair. Add a tee shirt and pants. Draw shoes. Erase extra lines.

8 Look closely at the bicycle frame. Draw the front part and handlebars.

9 Draw lines for the seat and rear frame.

48

10 Look at the wheels. Draw the wheels. Add a pedal under the boy's shoe.

11 Look at the final drawing. Add details. Shade and color your bicyclist.

Reader

Reading is one of my favorite things to do! This will give us a chance to draw a person sitting down.

1 This face will be in 3/4 view. Start with an egg for the head.

2 Notice that the eyes are drawn looking down. Draw the face. Add an ear. Draw lines for the neck.

3 Draw the chest trapezoid.

4 Notice the slight angle of the second trapezoid. Draw it.

5 Draw ovals for the upper arms and legs.

6 Look at the position of the lower arm. Draw it. Add the hand. Draw the lower leg ovals.

7 Look closely at the reader. Notice the way she is holding her book. Starting at the top, draw her hair. Draw the book. Draw lines for fingers. Draw feet. Erase extra lines.

8 She's sitting on a comfortable stool. Draw it. What other details do you see? Add these.

9 Shade and color your reader.

I wonder what she's reading. What's your favorite book?

Wheelchair basketball

This boy is disabled. He can't use his legs like other people. But, it doesn't stop him from playing basketball. He's a free-throw whiz!

1 Start with an egg.

2 Draw the face and an ear. Add the neck.

3 Draw the chest trapezoid.

4 Finish the body with a second trapezoid.

5 He will be whizzing about in his wheelchair. Look at the position of his upper arm and leg ovals. Draw these.

6 Look at his raised arms and hands. Draw the lower arms and hands. Look at his feet. Draw the feet.

7 Add hair. Draw a tee-shirt. Draw the beginning of the wheelchair. Erase extra lines.

8 Look again at details. Draw his uniform. Finish the wheelchair by adding the wheels.

9 Look at the final drawing. Finish his team uniform. Add a basketball. Shade and color the basketball player.

Girl climbing

Sometimes it's fun to just play. This girl is playing on a climber at the park.

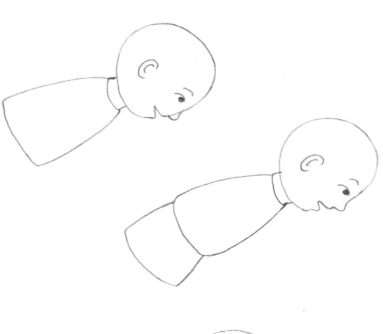

1 Look at the angle of the head. Start with an egg for the head.

2 Draw the face, nose and ear. Draw a neck.

3 Look at the angle of the chest. Add the chest.

4 Draw the lower torso. Erase extra lines to complete the face.

5 Look at the upper arm and leg ovals. Draw these

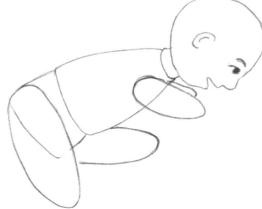

4 Draw the lower arm and leg ovals.

5 Look at the shapes that form her hands and feet. Add these.

6 Draw hair. Add clothes and shoes. Erase extra lines.

Now, let's draw her jumping down the climber.

Girl jumping

1 Start with an egg.

2 Draw the face. Draw an ear.
Add the neck.

3 Draw the chest.

4 Finish the body with a
second trapezoid.

5 Look at the angle of her
upper arm and leg ovals.
Draw these.

6 Look at the angles of the lower arm and leg ovals. Add these.

7 Draw hands and feet.

8 Erase extra lines. Add hair and clothes.

59

This girl is having fun playing on the climber at the park. Look at the shape of the climber. Draw it. Now draw the girl again, climbing up and jumping down.

Artist

Let's draw a picture of someone drawing a picture!

1 Start with an egg.

2 Add ears and a neck. This will be the back of her head.

3 Draw the torso.

4 Finish the body with a second trapezoid.

5 Look at the angles of the arm and leg ovals. Draw these.

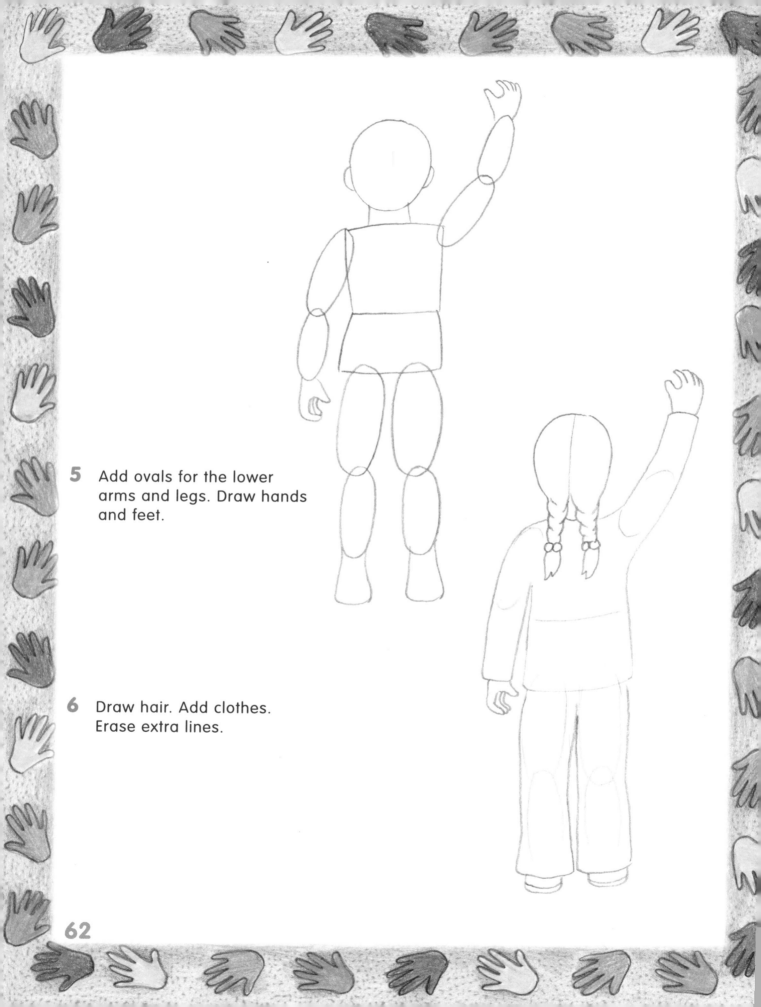

5 Add ovals for the lower arms and legs. Draw hands and feet.

6 Draw hair. Add clothes. Erase extra lines.

7 Look at her drawing. Finish and color your artist.

8 Draw the front view.

Awesome artist, just like you!

Index

Learn about other
drawing books online:
www.123draw.com